G. SCHIRMER'S
COLLECTION OF
OPERA LIBRETTO'S

MACBETH

Opera in Four Acts

Music by

Giuseppe Verdi

Libretto by
FRANCESCO MARIA PIAVE and ANDREA MAFFEI
(Based on Shakespeare's Play)

English Translation by
GLEN SAULS

Ed. 2520

G. SCHIRMER, *Inc.*

DISTRIBUTED BY
HAL•LEONARD®
CORPORATION
7777 W. BLUEMOUND RD. P.O. BOX 13819 MILWAUKEE, WI 53213

Important Notice

Performances of this opera must be licensed by the publisher.

All rights of any kind with respect to this opera and any parts thereof, including but not limited to stage, radio, television, motion picture, mechanical reproduction, translation, printing, and selling are strictly reserved.

License to perform this work, in whole or in part, whether with instrumental or keyboard accompaniment, must be secured in writing from the Publisher. Terms will be quoted upon request.

Copying of either separate parts or the whole of this work, by hand or by any other process, is unlawful and punishable under the provisions of the U.S.A. Copyright Act.

The use of any copies, including arrangements and orchestrations, other than those issued by the Publisher, is forbidden.

All inquiries should be directed to the Publisher:

G. Schirmer Rental Department
5 Bellvale Road
Chester, NY 10918
(914) 469-2271

MACBETH

Of all Verdi's operas of which there are two or more versions (*Don Carlo* boasts three), the most significant changes the composer ever made were in *Macbeth*. This opera, his tenth, remains noteworthy among Verdi's early works for more than one reason. It was the first manifestation of his profound love for Shakespeare and also his first attempt at music drama.

At the age of thirty-three, Verdi continued to write in the *bel canto* tradition of Bellini and Donizetti. In *Macbeth* his innate genius asserted itself for the first time in spite of frequent reliance on conventional devices.

Verdi took great pains with *Macbeth,* displaying special enthusiasm for it and an affection that endured long after, even though unshared by the public of his time. The composer himself sketched the first draft of the libretto before turning it over to Francesco Maria Piave for the finished verses. The resulting text stays close to the play, though much cutting and some transposition of order was necessary to suit operatic needs. Still not satisfied, Verdi turned to the poet-aristocrat Andrea Maffei to rewrite the witches' chorus and sleepwalking scene.

In revising the work extensively, the composer added much new music twenty years after the 1847 original.

Macbeth in Verdi's setting first took to the stage at the Teatro della Pergola, Florence, on March 14, 1847. Felice Varesi played the title role, with Marianna Barbieri Nini as his Lady and the composer serving as musical director. The first performance of the opera in America took place at Niblo's Gardens, New York, three years later, April 24, 1850.

The revived and improved version failed in Paris on April 21, 1865. Perhaps audiences by that time no longer favored the composer's earlier style and wanted "grander" operas, though he had conciliated them by adding a ballet in the scene of the apparitions.

The Metropolitan introduced the work to the company's repertory for the first time on February 5, 1959, with Leonard Warren creating his last role as Macbeth.

Courtesy of Opera News

THE STORY

ACT I. Macbeth and Banquo, generals in the army of King Duncan of Scotland, meet a band of witches while crossing a barren heath. These hags prophetically hail Macbeth as Thane of Cawdor and future king and Banquo as father of kings thereafter; no sooner have they vanished than messengers from Duncan approach, proclaiming Macbeth the new Thane of Cawdor. Amazed at this turn of events, Macbeth muses on his chances of gaining the crown.

In the great hall of her castle, Lady Macbeth reads a letter from her husband describing his meeting with the witches. Exulting in the prospect of power, she vows to add her own cunning and boldness to Macbeth's ambition. When a servant brings word that the king will spend the night in the castle, she invokes infernal powers to aid her aims. Macbeth enters and his wife persuades him to murder Duncan that very night. Just then Duncan and his train arrive; they retire at once. Macbeth, dreading his task, imagines a bloody dagger before his eyes. As a night bell sounds, he steals into the royal bedchamber. Lady Macbeth reenters; almost immediately her husband staggers from the room to tell her the deed is done. Seeing the dagger still in his hands, she coolly takes the weapon from him and goes to smear blood on the royal guards, who have been drugged. There is a knock at the gate; when Lady Macbeth returns, the couple withdraws. Macduff and Banquo enter, discover the murder and immediately summon the entire court, which invokes God's vengeance.

ACT II. Not satisfied with their uneasy throne, Macbeth and his wife plot the murder of Banquo and his son, lest the latter one day gain the crown. As her husband hurries off to arrange the crime, Lady Macbeth reaffirms their faith in the knife.

A group of assassins awaits Banquo in a deserted park; they withdraw as he enters with son Fleance. Troubled by a foreboding of evil, Banquo is set upon and killed, but the boy escapes.

In a magnificent banquet hall, Lady Macbeth toasts her guests in a brilliant drinking song. Macbeth secretly informed that the murder has been done, complains to the assembly of Banquo's absence. Suddenly, to the guests' astonishment, he imagines he sees the general's ghost seated at the table. Lady Macbeth chides her husband, and he momentarily regains his calm as she sings a reprise of the drinking song. But the bloody specter continues to haunt him; as the shocked guests comment on his guilty behavior, Lady Macbeth rebukes him for cowardice.

ACT III. In a cave eerie with disembodied heads, the witches stir their caldron. Macbeth enters to learn his fate, and at his insistence they conjure up a series of apparitions. The first, a warrior's head, tells him to beware Macduff; the second, a bloody child, assures him that no man born of woman can harm him; finally, a crowned child reveals that he will rule invincible till Birnam Wood marches against him. Somewhat reassured, he asks the witches if Banquo's sons will ever reign in Scotland; in reply, they invoke the spirits of eight kings, who pass before the terrified Macbeth. The last of the line is Banquo, holding a mirror that reflects the other kings. As Macbeth faints in dread, the witches disappear.

ACT IV. Near Birnam Wood a band of Scottish refugees bewail their oppressed homeland, caught in the bloody grip of Macbeth's tyranny. Macduff grieves over his murdered wife and children. He is joined by Malcolm, who instructs their soldiers to cut branches from the forest as camouflage for an attack on Macbeth's castle. The two leaders unite with the crowd in a call to arms.

A physician and lady-in-waiting observe the guilt-wracked Lady Macbeth as she wanders through the castle in her sleep, wiping imaginary bloodstains from her hands.

On a battlefield near the castle, Macbeth clings to the hope that he can withstand the forces of Malcolm and Macduff, but he is soul-weary and curses his fate. Word of his wife's death reaches him just as messengers bring the astounding news that Birnam Wood is advancing toward him; Macbeth leads his men to battle. Macduff seeks out Macbeth and, crying that he was not born of woman but torn prematurely from his mother's womb, fells the tyrant with his sword. Dying, Macbeth curses the day he heeded the witches' prophecies. Followed by a joyous crowd, the victorious Malcolm enters with his army; all give thanks for the deliverance of Scotland.

Courtesy of Opera News

CAST OF CHARACTERS

MACBETH, Thane of Cawdor . . . . *Baritone*

LADY MACBETH . . . . *Soprano*

BANQUO, a Scottish general . . . . *Bass*

MACDUFF, a Scottish nobleman . . . . *Tenor*

MALCOLM, son of King Duncan . . . . *Tenor*

LADY-IN-ATTENDANCE to Lady Macbeth . . . . *Soprano*

A PHYSICIAN . . . . *Bass*

A MURDERER . . . . *Baritone*

THREE APPARITIONS {
A Warrior . . . . *Baritone*
A Bloody Child . . . . *Soprano*
A Crowned Child . . . . *Soprano*
}

A MANSERVANT . . . . *Bass*

King Duncan, Fleance (son of Banquo), Attendants, Messengers, Soldiers, Assassins, Witches, Lords and Ladies, Scottish Refugees.

SYNOPSIS OF SCENES

MACBETH

ATTO I

SCENA 1: BOSCO

(Tre trocchi di Streghe appariscono l'un dopo l'altro fra lampi e tuoni.)

III
Che faceste? Dite su!

II
Ho sgozzato un verro!

III
E tu?

I
M'è frullata nel pensier
La mogliera d'un nocchier;
Al dimòn la mi cacciò.
Ma lo sposo che salpò
Col suo legno affogherò.

III
Un rovajo io ti darò . . .

II
I marosi io leverò . . .

I
Per le secche lo trarrò.
(Odesi un tamburo.)

TUTTE
Un tamburo! Che sarà?
Vien Macbetto. Eccolo qua!

(Si confondono insieme e intrecciano una ridda.)

Le sorelle vagabonde
Van per l'aria, van sull'onde,
Sanno un circolo intrecciare
Che comprende e terra e mar.

(Le Streghe vanno attorno danzando. Entra Macbeth e Banco.)

MACBETH
Giorno non vidi mai sì fiero e bello!

BANCO
Nè tanto glorioso!

MACBETH
(S'avvede delle Streghe.) Oh, chi saran costor?

BANCO
Chi siete voi? Di questo mondo
O d'altra regione?
Dirvi donne vorrei, ma lo mi vieta
Quella sordida barba.

MACBETH
Or via parlate!

STREGHE
(in tuono profetico)

III
Salve, o Macbetto, di Glamis Sire!

II
Salve, o Macbetto, di Caudor Sire!

I
Salve, o Macbetto, di Scozia Re!
(Macbeth trema.)

BANCO *(a Macbeth)*
Tremar vi fanno così lieti auguri?

(alle Streghe)

Favellate a me pur, se non v' è scuro,
Creature fantastiche, il futuro.

STREGHE

III
Salve!

II
Salve!

I
Salve!

III
Men sarai di Macbetto eppur maggiore!

II
Non quanto lui, ma più di lui felice!

I
Non Re, ma di Monarchi genitore!

TUTTE
Macbetto e Banco vivano!
Banco e Macbetto vivano!
(Spariscono.)

MACBETH
Vanir! . . . Saranno i figli tuoi sovrani.

1

MACBETH

ACT I

SCENE 1: A BARREN HEATH

(*Three covins of Witches appear one after the other amidst thunder and lightning.*)

THIRD GROUP OF WITCHES
What have you been doing? Tell us!

SECOND
I slit the throat of a boar.

THIRD
And you?

FIRST
I am brooding over a steerman's wife; she sent me to the devil. But her husband has set sail and I shall drown both ship and him.

THIRD
I'll give you a North wind . . .

SECOND
I shall raise the billows . . .

FIRST
I will cast him on a shoal.
(*A drum is heard.*)

ALL
A drum! What next?
Macbeth is coming. Behold, he is here!
(*They swarm together and tangle themselves in a whirling dance.*)
The roaming sisters, fleeting through skies, flitting over oceans, can weave a circle that includes both earth and sea.
(*The witches whirl in a dance. Enter Macbeth and Banquo.*)

MACBETH
I have never seen a day so wild and fine.

BANQUO
Nor so glorious!

MACBETH
(*catching sight of the Witches*)
Oh, who are they?

BANQUO
What are you? Of this world or from some other region? I would call you women but I am put off by those ragged beards.

MACBETH
Now speak!

WITCHES
(*in prophetic tone*)

THIRD GROUP OF WITCHES
Hail, O Macbeth, Thane of Glamis!

SECOND
Hail, O Macbeth, Thane of Cawdor!

FIRST
Hail, O Macbeth, King of Scotland!
(*Macbeth starts.*)

BANQUO
(*to Macbeth*)
Do you start at such words of happy augury?
(*to the Witches*)
Speak to me then, fantastic creatures, if the future is not unknown to you.

THIRD GROUP OF WITCHES
Hail!

SECOND
Hail!

FIRST
Hail!

THIRD
Less you will be than Macbeth, but greater!

SECOND
Not so happy as he, yet much more so!

FIRST
No king, but the father of kings!

ALL
Macbeth and Banquo, hail!
Hail, Banquo and Macbeth
(*They disappear.*)

MACBETH
Vanished! . . . Your children shall be kings.

1

BANCO

E tu Re pria di loro.

BANCO E MACBETH

Accenti arcani!

(*Entrano i Messaggeri del Re.*)

MESSAGGERI

Pro Macbetto! Il tuo signore
Sir t'elesse di Caudore.

MACBETH

Ma quel Sire ancor vi regge!

MESSAGGERI

No! percosso dalla legge
Sotto il ceppo egli spirò.

BANCO (*da sè*)

(Ah, l'inferno il ver parlò!)

MACBETH (*fra sè*)

Due vaticini compiuti or sono . . .
Mi si promette dal terzo un trono . . .
Ma perchè sento rizzarsi il crine?
Pensier di sangue, d'onde sei nato? . . .
Alla corona che m'offre il fato
La man rapace non alzerò.

BANCO (*fra sè*)

Oh, come s'empie costui d'orgoglio
Nella speranza d'un regio soglio!
Ma spesso l'empio Spirto d'averno
Parla, e c'inganna, veraci detti,
E ne abbandona poi maledetti
Su quell' abisso che ci scavò.

MESSAGGERI

Perchè sì freddo n'udì Macbetto?
Perchè l' aspetto non serenò?

(*Tutti partono. Le Streghe ritornano.*)

CORO DI STREGHE

S'allontanarono! . . . N'accozzeremo
Quando di fulmini . . . lo scroscio
    udremo.
S'allontanarono . . . fuggiam . . .
    s'attenda
Le sorti a compiere . . . nella tregenda.
Macbetto riedere . . . vedrem colà,
E il nostro oracolo . . . gli parlerà.

(*Partono.*)

SCENA 2: ATRIO NEL CASTELLO DI MAC-
BETH, CHE METTE IN ALTRE STANZE.

(*Entra Lady Macbeth leggendo una
lettera.*)

LADY MACBETH

"Nel dì della vittoria io le incontrai . . .
"Stupito io n' era per le udite cose;
"Quando i nunzi del Re mi salutaro
"Sir di Caudore; vaticinio uscito
"Dalle veggenti stesse
"Che predissero un serto al capo mio.
"Racchiudi in cor questo segreto.
                                Addio."
Ambizioso spirto
Tu sei Macbetto . . . Alla grandezza
    aneli,
Ma sarai tu malvagio?
Pien di misfatti è il calle
Della potenza, e mal per lui che il piede
Dubitoso vi pone, e retrocede!
    Vieni! t'affretta! accendere
    Ti vo' quel freddo core!
    L'audace impresa a compiere
    Io ti darò valore;
    Di Scozia a te promettono
    Le profetesse il trono.
    Che tardi? accetta il dono,
    Ascendivi a regnar.

(*Entra un Servo.*)

SERVO

Al cader della sera il Re qui giunge.

LADY MACBETH

Che dì? Macbetto è seco?

SERVO

Ei l'accompagna.
La nuova, o donna, è certa.

LADY MACBETH

Trovi accoglienza, quale un Re si merta.

(*Il Servo parte.*)

Duncano sarà qui? . . . qui? qui la
    notte?
    Or tutti sorgete,—ministri infernali,
    Che al sangue incorate—spingete i
        mortali!
    Tu notte ne avvolgi—di tenebra im-
        mota;
    Qual petto percota—non vegga il
        pugnal.

(*Entra Macbeth.*)

MACBETH

Oh donna mia!

LADY MACBETH

Caudore!

BANQUO
And you shall be king before them.

BANQUO AND MACBETH
Mysterious utterances!
(*Enter Messengers from the King.*)

MESSENGERS
Valiant Macbeth! Your sovereign
has made you Thane of Cawdor.

MACBETH
But that Thane still lives!

MESSENGERS
No. Struck down by the law,
he perished on the block.

BANQUO (*aside*)
(Ah, the devil speaks true then.)

MACBETH (*to himself*)
Two prophecies are thus fulfilled . . .
The third promised me a throne . . .
But why do I feel my hair standing
on end?
These bloody thoughts, from what
are they born?
I will not raise a grasping hand
to the crown that Fate offers me.

BANQUO (*aside*)
Oh, see how that man is filled with
pride by the hope of a royal throne!
But often the spirit of hell, in order to
deceive, speaks true and afterwards
abandons us, accursed, in that
abyss which it has dug for us.

MESSENGERS
Why did Macbeth receive our news so
coldly? Why does he not look better
satisfied?
(*They all leave. The Witches return.*)

CHORUS OF WITCHES
They have all gone! . . . We will gather
when next we hear the rumble of
thunder.
They are gone! . . . Let us flee . . .
Take care to fulfill the prophecies
. . . of our witches' troop.
Macbeth will return . . . we'll see him
there
and our oracle . . . shall speak to him.
(*Exeunt.*)

SCENE 2: A HALL IN MACBETH'S CASTLE
WITH SEVERAL ROOMS LEADING OFF
IT.
(*Lady Macbeth enters, reading a
letter.*)

LADY MACBETH
"On the day of victory I met them . . .
I stood in wonder at the things I
heard when messengers from the
King greeted me as Thane of Cawdor, as had been foretold by those
same prophets who predicted a crown
upon my brows. Enclose this secret
in your heart. Farewell."
An ambitious spirit is yours, Macbeth
. . . You long for greatness but would
you do wrong for it? Full of misdeeds
is the path to power, and woe to him
who sets his foot upon it doubtfully
and then retreats!
Come, then! Hasten! That I may
enflame that cold heart of yours!
Boldness is needed to complete this
task. I will give you courage. The
prophetesses have promised the
throne of Scotland to you. Why so
reluctant? Accept the gift, arise to
reign!
(*Enter a Servant.*)

SERVANT
At nightfall the King arrives here.

LADY MACBETH
What do you say? Is Macbeth with
him?

SERVANT
He accompanies him.
The news, my lady, is definite.

LADY MACBETH
He shall find the welcome here that a
King deserves.
(*Exit Servant.*)
Duncan will be here? . . . Here? Here
for the night? Now all you infernal
ministers arise, who incite to blood-
shed . . . who induce men to murder!
O, night, enshroud us . . . with dark-
est shadows, so that the dagger may
not see . . . the breast it strikes.
(*Enter Macbeth.*)

MACBETH
Oh, my wife!

LADY MACBETH
Cawdor!

MACBETH

Fra poco il Re vedrai . . .

LADY MACBETH

E partirà?

MACBETH

Domani.

LADY MACBETH

Mai non ci rechi il sole un tal domani.

MACBETH

Che parli?

LADY MACBETH

E non intendi? . . .

MACBETH

Intendo, intendo!

LADY MACBETH

Or bene?

MACBETH

E se fallisse il colpo?

LADY MACBETH

Non fallirà . . . se tu non tremi.

(lieti suoni che a poco si accostano)

Il Re!

Lieto or lo vieni ad incontrar con me.

(Partono.)

(Musica villereccia, la quale avazando
    si a poco a poco annuncia l'arrivo
    del Re. Egli trapassa accompagnato
    da Banco, Macduff, Malcolm, Mac-
    beth, Lady Macbeth e seguito.)

(Entra Macbeth e un Servo.)

MACBETH

Sappia la sposa mia, che pronta appena
La mia tazza notturna,
Vo' che un tocco di squilla a me lo
    avvisi.

(Il Servo parte.)

Mi si affaccia un pugnal?! L'elsa a me
    volta?!
Se larva non sei tu, ch'io ti brandisca.
Mi sfuggi . . . eppur ti veggo! A me
    precorri
Sul confuso cammin che nella mente
Di seguir disegnava! . . . Orrenda im-
    ago! . . .
Solco sanguigno la tua lama irriga! . . .

Ma nulla esista ancora . . . Il sol cruento
Mio pensier le dà forma, e come vera
Mi presenta allo sguardo una chimera.
Sulla metà del mondo
Or morta è la natura: or l'assassino
Come fantasma per l'ombre si striscia:
Or consuman le streghe i lor misteri.
Immobil terra! a' passi miei sta muta!

(Un tocco di squillo.)

È deciso . . . quel bronzo ecco m'invita!
Non udirlo, Duncano! È squillo eterno
Che nel cielo ti chiama, o nell' inferno.

(Entra nella stanza del Re. Entra Lady
    Macbeth sola lentamente.)

LADY MACBETH

Regna il sonno su tutti . . . Oh, qual
    lamento!
Risponde il gufo al suo lugubre addio!

MACBETH (di dentro)

Chi v' ha?

LADY MACBETH

Ch' ei fosse di letargo uscito
Pria del colpo mortal?

(Entra Macbeth barcollando e stravolto
    con un pugnale in mano.)

MACBETH

Tutto è finito!

(Si avvicina a Lady Macbeth.)

Fatal mia donna! un murmure
Com' io non intendesti?

LADY MACBETH

Del gufo udii lo stridere . . .
Testè che mai dicesti?

MACBETH

Io?

LADY MACBETH

Dianzi udirti parvemi.

MACBETH

Mentre io scendea?

LADY MACBETH

Sì!

MACBETH

Di'! nella stanza attigua
Chi dorme?

LADY MACBETH

Il regal figlio . . .

MACBETH

(guardandosi le mani)

O vista, o vista orribile!

MACBETH

Soon you shall see the King . . .

LADY MACBETH

When does he leave?

MACBETH

Tomorrow.

LADY MACBETH

May the sun not bring forth such a tomorrow.

MACBETH

What do you say?

LADY MACBETH

Do you not understand? . . .

MACBETH

I understand, I understand!

LADY MACBETH

Well then?

MACBETH

And what if the stroke should fail?

LADY MACBETH

It will not fail . . . if you do not shrink.

(*distant music which gradually draws nearer*)

The King!

Now joyfully come with me to meet him.

(*Exeunt.*)

(*The sound of rustic music drawing nearer announces the arrival of the King. He passes across the scene accompanied by Banquo, Macduff, Malcolm, Macbeth, Lady Macbeth and Attendants.*)

(*Enter Macbeth with a Servant.*)

MACBETH

Tell my wife that as soon as my nightly cup has been prepared I am to be informed by a stroke upon the bell.

(*Exit Servant.*)

Is this a dagger that appears to me? Its handle towards me?! If you are not a vision, let me brandish you . . . It flees from me . . . again I see you! You go before me down the tangled path I had in mind and was resolved to follow! . . . Horrid specter! . . . A furrow of blood waters your blade! . . . Again there is nothing . . . My bloody

thoughts alone created it, and, as if it were the truth, present to my sight this phantom. Now over one half of the world nature is dead: now the assassin stalks like a specter through the darkness. Now witches consummate their rites. Immobile earth! Let my footsteps be silent!

(*A bell rings.*)

It is settled . . . Behold, the bell invites me!

Do not hear it, Duncan! It is the knell That summons you to Heaven or to Hell.

(*He goes into the King's chamber. Lady Macbeth slowly enters alone.*)

LADY MACBETH

Sleep reigns over all . . . Oh, what a cry! The owl is answering to his sad farewell.

MACBETH (*within*)

Who is there?

LADY MACBETH

Can he perchance have shaken off his sleep before the fatal stroke?

(*Macbeth enters reeling and distraught, a dagger in his hand.*)

MACBETH

All is done.

(*approaching Lady Macbeth*)

Oh fateful wife! Did you hear a murmur, as I did?

LADY MACBETH

I heard the cry of an owl . . . but what did you say?

MACBETH

I?

LADY MACBETH

I thought I heard you speak.

MACBETH

As I came down the stairs?

LADY MACBETH

Yes!

MACBETH

Tell me! Who sleeps in the adjacent room?

LADY MACBETH

The royal prince . . .

MACBETH

(*looking at his hands*)

What a sight, what a horrid sight!

LADY MACBETH

Storna da questo il ciglio.

MACBETH

Nel sonno udii che oravano
I Cortigiani, e: *Dio
Sempre ne assista,* ei dissero;
Amen dir volli anch' io,
Ma la parola indocile
Gelò sui labbri miei.

LADY MACBETH

Follie!

MACBETH

Perchè ripetere
Quell' *Amen* non potei?

LADY MACBETH

Follie, follie che sperdono
I primi rai del dì.

MACBETH

Allor questa voce m' intesi nel petto:
"Avrai per guanciali sol vepri, o Mac-
betto!
Il sonno per sempre, Glamis, uccidesti!
Non v'è che vigilia, Caudore, per te!"

LADY MACBETH

Ma dimmi, altra voce non parti d'
udire?
"Sei vano, o Macbetto, ma privo
d'ardire;
Glamis, a mezz' opra vacilli, t'arresti;
Fanciul vanitoso, Caudore, tu se'!"

MACBETH

Com' angeli d' ira, vendetta tuonarmi,
Udrò di Duncano le sante virtù.

LADY MACBETH

(Quell animo trema, combatte, delira..
Chi mai lo direbbe l' invitto che fu!)
Il pugnal là riportate . . .
Le sue guardie insanguinate . . .
Che l'accusa in lor ricada.

MACBETH

Io colà . . . non posso entrar!

LADY MACBETH

Dammi il ferro.
(*Strappa dalli mani di Macbeth il pug-
nale, ed entra nelle stanze del Re.—
Bussano forte alla porta del castello.*)

MACBETH

Ogni rumore mi spaventa! (*Si guarda
le mani.*)
Oh, questa mano . . .
Non potrebbe l' Oceano
Queste mani a me lavar.
(*Entra Lady Macbeth.*)

LADY MACBETH

Ve'! le mani ho lorde anch' io;
Poco spruzzo, e monde son.
L' opra anch'essa andrà in obblio . . .

MACBETH

Odi tu? raddoppia il suon!

LADY MACBETH

Vieni altrove! ogni sospetto
Rimoviam dall' uccisor;
Torna in te, fa cor Macbetto!
Non ti vinca un vil timor.

MACBETH

Oh potessi il mio delitto
Dalla mente cancellar!
Oh potessi, o Re trafitto,
L'alto sonno a te spezzar!
(*Macbeth è trascinato via da Lady
Macbeth. Entra Macduff e Banco.*)

MACDUFF

Di destarlo per tempo il Re m' impose;
E di già tarda è l' ora.
Qui m' attendete, o Banco.
(*Entra nelle stanze del Re.*)

BANCO

Oh qual orrenda notte!
Per l'aer cieco lamentose voci,
Voci s' udian di morte . . .
Gemea cupo l' augel de' tristi auguri,
E della terra si sentì il tremore . . .
(*Macduff entra aggitatissimo.*)

MACDUFF

Orrore! orrore! orrore!

BANCO

Che avenne mai?

MACDUFF

Là dentro
Contemplate voi stesso . . . io dir nol
posso!
(*Banco entra precipitoso nelle stanze
del Re.*)
Correte! . . . olà . . . tutti correte! tutti!
O delitto! o delitto! o tradimento!

LADY MACBETH

Turn your eyes away from it.

MACBETH

I heard the courtiers praying in their sleep; and they said "May God protect us always." I wanted to say "Amen," but the stubborn word froze on my lips.

LADY MACBETH

This is madness!

MACBETH

Why couldn't I pronounce that "Amen"?

LADY MACBETH

Madness, this is madness that the dawn's first rays will quite dispel.

MACBETH

And then I heard this voice within my breast:
"Henceforth your pillows shall be as briars to you, Macbeth!
Glamis has murdered sleep forever!
Nothing but wakeful nights for you, Cawdor!"

LADY MACBETH

But tell me, did you hear no other voice that said:
"You are proud, Macbeth, but lack courage.
Glamis, in mid-task you hesitate, you stop.
Cawdor, you are vain and womanish"?

MACBETH

With the wrath of angels the holy virtue of Duncan cries out for vengeance.

LADY MACBETH

(His soul is in torment, it struggles, it raves . . . What would one say now of the once unconquerable hero?)
Take back the dagger . . . smear the guards with blood . . . so that the blame may fall on them.

MACBETH

I cannot go in there again!

LADY MACBETH

Give me the knife.
(*She snatches the dagger from Macbeth and goes into the King's chamber. There are loud knocks on the gate of the castle.*)

MACBETH

Every sound alarms me.
(*He looks at his hands.*)
Oh, these hands . . .
The ocean would not be able
to cleanse these hands for me.
(*Enter Lady Macbeth.*)

LADY MACBETH

See, my hands are stained like yours; a sprinkling of water and they'll be clean again. The deed itself will thus be obliterated . . .

MACBETH

Do you hear? The sound gets louder!

LADY MACBETH

Come away with me! We must remove all suspicion of the murder. Control yourself, be bold, Macbeth! Do not let base fears overcome you.

MACBETH

Would I were able to put my crime from mind. Would I were able, O murdered King, to treat your deep sleep lightly!
(*Lady Macbeth draws him off. Macduff and Banquo enter.*)

MACDUFF

The King instructed me to wake him betime. Already it is getting late. Wait for me here, Banquo.
(*He goes into the King's chamber.*)

BANQUO

Oh, what a frightful night! Through the choking air were heard wailing voices prophesying death . . . The bird of ill-omen croaked gloomily and the earth was felt to shudder.
(*Macduff enters, greatly agitated.*)

MACDUFF

Oh horror! Horror! Horror!

BANQUO

What is the matter?

MACDUFF

Go in and see it for yourself . . . I cannot speak it!
(*Banquo rushes into the King's chamber.*)
Help! . . . Awake . . . Everyone run here! All!
Oh, murder! Murder! Oh, treason!

(*Entrano frettolosi Macbeth, Lady Macbeth, Malcolm, Dama di Lady Macbeth e Servi.*)

MACBETH E LADY MACBETH

Qual subito scompiglio!

BANCO (*entra in scena*)

Oh noi perduti!

TUTTI

Che fu? parlate! che seguì di strano?

BANCO

È morto assassinato il Re Duncano!!

TUTTI

Schiudi, inferno, la bocca ed inghiotti
Nel tuo grembo l'intero creato;
Sull'ignoto assissino esecrato
Le tue fiamme discendano, o ciel.
O gran Dio, che ne' cuori penetri,
Tu ne assisti, in te solo fidiamo;
Da te lume, consiglio cerchiamo
A squarciar delle tenebre il vel!
L'ira tua formidabile e pronta
Colga l'empio, o fatal punitor;
E vi stampa sul volto l'impronta
Che stampasti sul primo uccisor.

ATTO II

SCENA 1: STANZA NEL CASTELLO

(*Macbeth pensoso e Lady Macbeth.*)

LADY MACBETH

Perchè mi sfuggi, e fiso
Ognor ti veggo in un pensier profondo?
Il fatto è irreparabile. Veraci
Parlar le maliarde, e Re tu sei!
Il figlio di Duncan, per l'improvvisa
Sua fuga in Inghilterra.
Parracida fu detto, e vuoto il soglio
A te lasciò.

MACBETH

Ma le spirtali donne
Banco padre di regi han profetato . . .
Dunque i suoi figli regneran? Duncano
Per costor sarà spento?

LADY MACBETH

Egli e suo figlio vivono è ver . . .

MACBETH

Ma vita immortale non hanno . . .

LADY MACBETH

Ah sì, non l'hanno!

MACBETH

Forza è che scorra un altro sangue, o donna!

LADY MACBETH

Dove? Quando?

MACBETH

Al venir di questa notte.

LADY MACBETH

Immoto sarai tu nel tuo disegno?

MACBETH

Banco! l'eternità t'apre il suo regno.
(*Parte precipitoso.*)

LADY MACBETH

La luce langue, il faro spegnesi
Ch'eterno scorre per gl'ampi cieli!
Notte desiata, provvida veli
La man colpevole che ferirà.
Nuovo delitto!! . . . È necessario!
Compiersi debbe l'opra fatale.
Ai trapassati regnar non cale;
A loro un requiem, l'eternità! . . .
O voluttà del soglio! o scettro, alfin sei mio.
Ogni mortal desio tace e s'acqueta in te.
Cadrà fra poco esanime chi fu predetto Re.

SCENA 2: PARCO. IN LONTANANZA IL CASTELLO DI MACBETH.

CORO DI SICARI

I

Chi v'impose ùnirvi a noi?

II

Fu Macbetto.

I

Ed a che far?

II

Deggiam Banco trucidar.

I

Quando? . . . dove? . . .

II

Insiem con voi.
Con suo figlio ei qui verrà.

(*Enter in haste Macbeth, Lady Macbeth, Malcolm, Lady-in-waiting and attendants.*)

MACBETH and LADY MACBETH
What is this sudden uproar?

BANQUO (*entering*)
Oh, we are lost!

ALL
What is it? Speak! What strange thing has happened?

BANQUO
King Duncan is dead! Murdered!

ALL
Jaws of Hell, open wide and swallow all creation in your bowels; upon the unknown and accursed assassin throw down your flames of wrath, O heaven!
O God, who peerest into every heart, give us Thy aid. In Thee alone we trust; grant us Thy light. We seek Thy guidance to rend this shroud of darkness.
Let your tremendous wrath be prompt to strike the guilty one, O great Chastiser; and stamp upon his brows the mark with which you branded the first murderer.

ACT II

SCENE 1: A ROOM IN THE CASTLE

(*Macbeth, sunk in thought, and Lady Macbeth.*)

LADY MACBETH
Why do you shun me, and why do I always see you fixed in deep thought like this? What's done cannot be undone. The sorcerers spoke true, and you are King! Duncan's son, by the imprudence of his flight to England, is thought to be the guilty parricide and has left the throne vacant for you.

MACBETH
But the inspired women foretold that Banquo would be the sire of kings . . . ·
Therefore shall his sons reign?
Was Duncan killed for them?

LADY MACBETH
He and his son still live, 'tis true . . .

MACBETH
But they do not have immortal life . . .

LADY MACBETH
Ah yes, that they have not!

MACBETH
Other blood must flow, O my wife!

LADY MACBETH
Where? When?

MACBETH
This very night.

LADY MACBETH
Will you be constant in your purpose?

MACBETH
Banquo! Eternity opens its kingdom to you.
(*He hastens out.*)

LADY MACBETH
The light wanes as the dying lamp of heaven sinks
on its eternal journey through the skies!
This longed-for night provides a veil
for the guilty hand about to wound.
Another crime! . . . Yet it must be!
This fatal business must be carried out.
The dead have no desire to rule:
for them a lasting peace, eternity!
O ecstacy of royal glory! O scepter, at last you are mine,
At once you soothe and silence all mortal longings.
Before long, he who was predicted King shall fall lifeless.

SCENE 2: A PARK. IN THE DISTANCE MACBETH'S CASTLE IS VISIBLE.

CHORUS OF MURDERERS

FIRST
Who ordered you to join us?

SECOND
It was Macbeth.

FIRST
To do what?

SECOND
To kill Banquo.

FIRST
When? . . . Where? . . .

SECOND
With you.
We will find him here with his son.

I

Rimanete, or bene sta.

TUTTI

Sparve il sol! . . . la notte or regni
Scellerata . . . insanguinata;
Cieca notte, affretta e spegni
Ogni lume in terra, in ciel.
L'ora è presso! . . . or n'occultiamo.
Nel silenzio lo aspettiamo.
Trema, Banco! . . . nel tuo fianco
Sta la punta del coltel!

(Si ritirono. Entra Banco e Fleance.)

BANCO

Studia il passo, o mio figlio! . . . usciam
    da queste
Tenebre . . . un senso ignoto
Nascar mi sento in petto
Pien di tristo presagio e di sospetto.
Come dal ciel precipita
L'ombra più sempre oscura!
In notte ugual trafissero
Duncano il mio signor.
Mille affannose immagini
M' annunciano sventura,
E il mio pensiero ingombrano
Di larve e di terror.

(Si perdono nel parco; voce di Banco
    dentro la scena.)

Ohimè! . . . Fuggi, mio figlio! . . . o
    tradimento!

(Fleance attraversa la scena inseguito
    da un Sicario.)

SCENA 3: MAGNIFICA SALA. MENSA
IMBANDITA.

(Lady Macbeth, Macbeth, Macduff,
    Dame e Servi.)

CORO

Salve, o Re!

MACBETH

Voi pur salvete,
Nobilissimi Signori!

CORO

Salve, o donna!

LADY MACBETH

Ricevete
La mercè de' vostri onori.

MACBETH

Prenda ciascun l'orrevole
Seggio al suo grado eletto!
Pago son io d'accogliere
Tali ospiti a banchetto.
La mia consorte assidasi
Nel trono a lei sortito,
Ma pria le piaccio un brindisi
Sciogliere a vostr' onor.

LADY MACBETH

Al tuo regale invito
Son pronta, o mio Signor.

CORO

E tu ne udrai rispondere
Come ci detta il cor.

LADY MACBETH

Si colmi il calice
Di vino eletto;
Nasca il diletto,
Muoia il dolor.
Da noi s'involino
Gli odi e gli sdegni,
Folleggi e regni
Qui solo amor.
Gustiamo il balsamo
D'ogni ferita,
Che nuova vita
Ridona al cor.
Cacciam le torbide
Cure dal petto;
Nasca il diletto,
Muoia il dolor.

TUTTI

Cacciam le torbide
Cure dal petto;
Nasca il diletto,
Muoia il dolor.

(Un Sicario comparisce sulla porta:
    Macbeth gli si avvicina e gli dice sotto
    voce.)

MACBETH

Tu di sangue hai brutto il volto.

SICARIO

È di Bianco.

MACBETH

Il vero ascolto?

SICARIO

Sì.

MACBETH

Ma il figlio?

FIRST

All right. You may stay.

ALL

The sun has vanished! . . . Now the
night reigns over ill-deeds . . . blood-
shed; blind night, hurry and extin-
guish all light on earth and in the
sky. The hour grows late!. . . Now we
must hide ourselves. We shall await
them in silence. Tremble, Banquo!
. . . For in your ribs you shall find
the point of a knife!

(*They withdraw. Enter Banquo and
Fleance.*)

BANQUO

Be careful of your steps, my son! . . .
Let us hurry
from these gloomy shadows . . .
I feel a strange presentiment
being born within me,
full of suspicion and foreboding doom.
See how the shades of night descend.
The shadows grow deeper and darker.
Just such a night as this brought death
to Duncan, my sovereign lord.
Thousands of frightful specter shapes
seem to predict disaster
and burden my soul with gloomy fears
of phantoms and unknown crimes.

(*They disappear into the woods; Banquo's voice is heard in the distance.*)

Help! . . . Fly, my son! . . . Oh,
treachery!

(*Fleance crosses the scene, pursued by
one of the Murderers.*)

SCENE 3: THE BANQUET HALL

*A banquet table is set. Lady Macbeth,
Macbeth, Macdoff, Lady Macbeth's
Lady-in-Attendance, Lords and
Ladies.*

CHORUS

Long live the King!

MACBETH

My warmest greetings to you,
most noble lords and ladies.

CHORUS

Long live the Queen!

LADY MACBETH

Receive my thanks
for the honor you do me.

MACBETH

Let each take the seat proper to his
rank.
I am content indeed to welcome
such guests to my table.
My consort will be seated
on the throne allotted to her.
But first I will ask her
to propose a toast in your honor.

LADY MACBETH

My lord, I am obedient
to your royal command.

CHORUS

And you shall hear us reply
most heartily.

LADY MACBETH

Fill the goblet to the brim
with choicest wine.
Let pleasure be born,
let sorrows die.
Have done with all hatred,
do away with all scorn.
Let only love
and jollity reign here.
Let us taste and enjoy
the cure of all ills,
that brings renewed life
to every heart.
Let us drive away the dull
cares of the soul;
Let pleasure be born
and sorrows die.

CHORUS

Let us drive away the dull
Cares of the soul;
Let pleasure be born
And sorrows die.

(*One of the Murderers appears at the
door. Macbeth goes over to him and
speaks in an aside.*)

MACBETH

You have blood stains upon your face.

MURDERER

They are Banquo's.

MACBETH

Do I hear the truth?

MURDERER

Yes.

MACBETH

But the boy?

SICARIO

Ne sfuggì.

MACBETH

Cielo! . . . ma Banco?

SICARIO

Egli morì.

(*Macbeth fa cenno al Sicario di partire.*)

LADY MACBETH

Che ti scosta, o re mio sposo,
Dalla gioia del banchetto? . . .

MACBETH

Banco falla! il valoroso
Chiuderebbe il serto eletto
A quant' avvi di più degno
Nell' intero nostro regno.

LADY MACBETH

Venir disse, e ci mancò.

MACBETH

In sua vece io sederò.

(*Macbeth va per sedere. Lo spettro di Banco, veduto solo da lui, ne occupa il posto.*)

Di voi chi ciò fece?

TUTTI

Che parli?

MACBETH (*allo spettro*)

Non dirmi ch'io fossi! . . . le ciocche cruenti
Non scuotermi incontro . . .

TUTTI (*con spavento*)

Macbetto è soffrente
Partiamo . . .

LADY MACBETH

Restate! Gli è morbo fugace . . .

(*a parte a Macbeth*)

E un uomo voi siete?

MACBETH

Lo sono, ed audace
S' io guardo tal cosa che al demone stesso
Farebbe spavento . . . là . . . là . . . nol ravvisi?

(*allo spettro*)

O poichè le chiome scrollar t'è concesso,
Favella! il sepolcro può render gli uccisi?

(*L'ombra sparisce.*)

LADY MACBETH

(*piano a Macbeth*)

Voi siete demente!

MACBETH

Quest' occhi l' han visto . . .

LADY MACBETH

Sedete, mio sposo! Ogn'ospite è tristo.
Svegliate la gioia!

MACBETH (*con calma*)

Ciascun mi perdoni!
Il brindisi lieto di nuovo risuoni,
Nè Banco obbliate, che lungi è tuttor.

LADY MACBETH

Si colmi il calice
Di vino eletto;
Nasca il diletto,
Muoia il dolor.
Da noi s'involino
Gli odi e gli sdegni,
Folleggi e regni
Qui solo amor.
Gustiamo il balsamo
D'ogni ferita
Che nuova vita
Ridona al cor.
Vuotiam per l'inclito
Banco i bicchieri!
Fior de' guerrieri,
Di Scozia onor.

TUTTI

Vuotiam per l'inclito
Banco i bicchieri!
Fior de' guerrieri,
Di Scozia onor.

(*Riappare lo Spettro.*)

MACBETH

(*spaventato*)

Va, spirto d' abisso! . . .
Spalanca una fossa.
O terra, l'ingoia . . . Fiammeggian quell'ossa!
Quel sangue fumante mi sbalza nel volto!
Quel guardo a me volto . . . trafiggemi il cor!

TUTTI

Sventura! terror!

MURDERER

He got away from us.

MACBETH

O heaven! . . . but Banquo?

MURDERER

He is dead.
(*Macbeth motions the Murderer to
    leave.*)

LADY MACBETH

Why do you absent yourself, my lord
    and King, from the joys of the
    feast?

MACBETH

Banquo has failed us! That valiant man
    would have completed the select
    circle of those who are the most
    worthy within our kingdom.

LADY MACBETH

He said he would come,
    and now we miss him.

MACBETH

I will sit in his vacant place.
(*Macbeth goes toward it. The Ghost
    of Banquo, seen only by him, oc-
    cupies the chair.*)
Which of you has done this?

CHORUS

What is he saying?

MACBETH (*to the Ghost*)

You cannot say I did it! . . . Do not
    shake you bloody locks towards . . .

ALL (*alarmed*)

Macbeth is ill.
Let us leave . . .

LADY MACBETH

Be seated! It is but a passing illness.
    (*to Macbeth*)
Are you a man?

MACBETH

I am, and a brave one if I can look
    upon that which would scare the
    devil himself . . . There . . . there
    . . . can you not see?
        (*to the Ghost*)
If it is given to you to shake your locks,
    then speak! Can sepulchres give up
    their dead?
        (*The Ghost disappears.*)

LADY MACBETH

(*to Macbeth*)
You are beside yourself!

MACBETH

With these eyes I saw him!

LADY MACBETH

My lord, be seated! All our guests are
    dismayed. Let joy and mirth return!

MACBETH (*calmly*)

Everyone pardon me.
Let the happy toast resound once more
    and let us not forget Banquo, who is
    still absent.

LADY MACBETH

Fill the goblet to the brim
with choicest wine.
Let pleasure be born,
let sorrows die.
Have done with all hatred,
do away with all scorn.
Let only love
and jollity reign here.
Let us taste and enjoy
the cure of all ills,
that brings renewed life
to every heart.
We'll empty our goblets
to the renowned Banquo!
Flower of warriors,
the glory of Scotland!

LADY-IN-ATTENDANCE, MACDUFF AND
CHORUS

We'll empty our goblets
To the renowned Banquo!
Flower of warriors,
The glory of Scotland!
(*The Ghost reappears.*)

MACBETH

(*in great alarm*)
Begone, spirit from Hell!
O Earth, gape open in a pit and swal-
    low him . . . consume those bones in
    flame!
That smoking blood does splatter on
    my face!
The look he gives me . . . it does trans-
    fix my heart!

ALL

O horror! O terror!

MACBETH

Quant' altri, io pur oso! . . .
Diventa pur tigre, leon minaccioso . . .
M'abbranca . . . Macbetto tremar non
vedrai,
Conoscer portrai . . . s' io provi
terror . . .
Ma fuggi! deh fuggi, fantasma tremen-
do!
(*L'ombra sparisce.*)
La vita riprendo!

LADY MACBETH
(*piano a Macbeth*)

Vergogna, signor!

MACBETH

Sangue a me quell' ombra chiede
E l'avrà, l'avrà, lo giuro!
Il velame del futuro
Alle Streghe squarcierò.

LADY MACBETH
(*a Macbeth*)

Spirto imbelle! il tuo spavento
Vane larve t' ha creato.
Il delitto è consumato;
Chi morì tornar non può.

MACDUFF (*fra sè*)

Biechi arcani! . . . s' abbandoni
Questa terra; or ch' ella è retta
Da una mano maledetta,
Viver solo il reo vi può.

TUTTI

Biechi arcani! sgomentato
Da fantasmi egli ha parlato!
Uno speco di ladroni
Questa terra diventò.

ATTO III

UN' OSCURA CAVERNA. NEL MEZZO UNA
CALDAIA CHE BOLLE; TUONI E LAMPI.

STREGHE

III
Tre volte miagola la gatta in fregola.

II
Tre volte l' upupa lamenta ed ulula.

I
Tre volte l' istrice guaisce al vento.
Questo è il momento.

TUTTI

Su via! sollecite giriam la pentola,
Mesciamvi in circolo possenti intingoli;
Sirocchie, all' opra! l' acqua già fuma,
Crepita, e spuma.

III
Tu rospo venefico,
Che suggi l' aconito,
Tu vepre, tu radica
Sbarbata al crepuscolo,
Va, cuoci gorgoglia
Nel vaso infernal.

II
Tu lingua di vipera,
Tu pelo di nottola,
Tu sangue di scimmia,
Tu dente di bottolo,
Va, bolli e t' avvoltola
Nel brodo infernal.

I
Tu dito d' un pargolo
Strozzato nel nascere,
Tu labbro d' un Tartaro,
Tu cor d' un eretico,
Va dentro, e consolida
La polta infernal.

TUTTI
(*danzando intorno*)

Bolli . . . bolli.
E voi Spirti
Negri e candidi,
Rossi e ceruli,
Rimescete!
Voi che mescete
Ben sapete
Rimescete!
Rimescete!
(*Entra Macbeth.*)

MACBETH
(*sull' ingresso, parlando ad alcuni
de'suoi*)

Finchè appelli, silenti m' attendete.
(*Si avanza verso le Streghe.*)
Che fate voi, misteriose donne?

STREGHE (*solenne*)
Un' opra senza nome.

MACBETH
Per quest' opra infernal io vi scongiuro!
Ch' io sappia il mio destin, se cielo e
terra
Dovessero innovar l' antica guerra.

MACBETH

I dare what others can! . . .
Come as a tiger or a threatening
  lion. . .
Seize me . . . you'll not see Macbeth
  tremble.
Then you will find out if I show
  fear . . .
But begone! Fly from here, ghastly
  phantom!

(*The Ghost disappears.*)

I can live again!

LADY MACBETH

(*aside, to Macbeth*)

For shame, my lord.

MACBETH

That spirit wants blood from me and
  it shall have it, it shall have it, I
  swear! The witches shall tear off for
  me the veil that hides the future.

LADY MACBETH

(*to Macbeth*)

Oh, cowardly spirit! Your fears have
  created empty specters. The dark
  deed is done; the dead cannot return.

MACDUFF (*aside*)

Guilty secrets! . . . I will quit this
  land: now that it is ruled by a cursed
  hand only the guilty can live in it.

ALL

Guilty secrets! Alarmed by phantoms,
  he has spoken! This country has be-
  come a den of criminals.

ACT III

THE WITCHES' CAVE

*A caldron is boiling in the middle of
the cave. Skull-like masks hang from
above.*

WITCHES
THIRD GROUP

Thrice a cat in heat has mewed.

SECOND

Thrice the hoopoe bird has shrieked
  and howled.

FIRST

Three times the porcupine has whined
  to the wind. This is the moment.

ALL

Let us begin. Hurry round the pot.
  Mix in a ring the potent brew; sisters, to work! Already the water
  steams, hisses and foams.

THIRD

Thou venomous toad
that sucks on wolfbane,
thou thorn, thou root of drug
plucked out at twilight,
go in, cook and gurgle
in the infernal pot.

SECOND

Thou tongue of viper,
thou skin of bat,
thou blood of an ape,
thou tooth of cur,
go in, boil and stew
in the infernal broth.

FIRST

Thou finger of an infant
strangled at its birth,
thou Tartar's lip,
thou heart of an heretic,
go in and thicken
our infernal brew.

ALL

(*dancing around the caldron*)

Boil . . . boil.
Now you spirits,
black and white,
red and blue,
stir, stir!
You who know well
how to mix,
stir!
Stir!

(*Enter Macbeth.*)

MACBETH

(*at the entrance, talking to some of his
  men*)

Await me in silence till I thee call.

(*coming toward the Witches*)

What are you doing, mysterious
  women?

WITCHES (*solemnly*)

A deed without a name.

MACBETH

By that infernal deed I conjure you!
I must know my future, even if heaven
  and earth renew their ancient war.

STREGHE

Dalle incognite Posse udir lo vuoi,
Cui ministre obbediam, oppur da noi?

MACBETH

Evocatele pur, se del futuro
Mi possono chiarir l' enigma oscuro.

STREGHE

Dalle basse e dall' alte regioni,
Spirti erranti, salite, scendete!
(*Scoppia un fulmine, e sorge una testa coperta d' elmo.*)

MACBETH

Dimmi o spirto . . .

STREGHE

T' ha letto nel core;
Taci, e n' odi le voci segrete.

APPARISCE

O Macbetto! Macbetto! Macbetto!
Da Macduffo ti guarda prudente.

MACBETH

Tu m' afforzi l' accolto sospetto!

(*all' ombra*)

Solo un motto . . .
(*Sparisce.*)

STREGHE

Richieste non vuole.
Ecco un altro di lui più possente.
(*Tuono: apparisce un fanciullo insanguinato.*)
Taci, e n'odi l'occulte parole.

APPARISCE

O Macbetto! Macbetto! Macbetto!
Esser puoi sanguinario, feroce:
Nessun nato di donna ti nuoce.
(*Sparisce.*)

MACBETH

O Macduffo, tua vita perdono . . .
No! . . . morrai! sul regale mio petto
Doppio usbergo sarà la tua morte!
(*Tuoni e lampi: sorge un fanciullo coronato che porta un arboscello.*)
Ma che avvisa quel lampo, quel tuono?. . .
Un fanciullo col serto dei Re!

STREGHE

Taci ed odi.

APPARISCE

Sta d' animo forte:
Glorioso, invincibil sarai
Fin che il bosco di Birnam vedrai
Ravviarsi e venir contro te!
(*Sparisce.*)

MACBETH

Oh! lieto augurio! Per magica possa
Selva alcuna giammai non fu mossa.
(*alle Streghe*)
Or mi dite: Salire al mio soglio
La progenie di Banco dovrà?

STREGHE

Non cercarlo!

MACBETH

Lo voglio! lo voglio!
O su voi la mia spada cadrà.
(*La caldaia cala sotterra.*)
La caldaia è sparita? perchè?
(*Suono sotteraneo di cornamusa.*)
Qual concento! Parlate! Che v' è?

STREGHE

III

Apparite!

II

Apparite!

I

Apparite!

TUTTI

Poi qual nebbia di nuovo sparite.
(*Otto Re passano uno dopo l'altro. L'ultimo, Banco, con uno specchio in mano.*)

MACBETH

(*al primo*)

Fuggi, regal fantasima,
Che Banco a me rammenti!
La tua corona è folgore,
Gli occhi mi fai roventi!
(*al secondo*)
Via, spaventosa immagine,
Che il crin di bende hai cinto!
(*agli altri*)
Ed altri ancor ne sorgono?
Un terzo? . . . un quarto? . . . un quinto?
Oh! mio terror! . . . dell' ultimo
Splende uno specchio in mano,
E nuovi Re s' attergano
Dentro al cristallo arcano . . .

WITCHES

Would you hear it from those unknown powers whom we, as ministers, obey, or else from us?

MACBETH

Invoke them straightway if they can reveal the dark secrets of the future to me.

WITCHES

From the depths and from on high, you wandering spirits arise, descend!

(*A clap of thunder and there arises a warrior's head, wearing a helmet.*)

MACBETH

Speak to me, Spirit . . .

WITCHES

It knows your thoughts; be still and listen to the secret voice.

APPARITION

O Macbeth! Macbeth! Macbeth! Beware of Macduff. Beware.

MACBETH

You confirm the suspicion that I had.

(*to the Specter*)

Just one word more . . .

(*It disappears.*)

WITCHES

He will not be commanded.
Lo, here is another, mightier than the first!

(*Thunder; a bloody child appears.*)

Be still and listen to the magic words.

APPARITION

O Macbeth! Macbeth! Macbeth!
You may be bloody and fierce, for no one born of woman can harm you.

(*It vanishes.*)

MACBETH

O Macduff, then I pardon your life . . .
No! . . . You shall die . . . Upon my royal breast your death shall be a double armor!

(*Thunder and lightning: there arises a crowned child bearing a green bough.*)

What does this lightning and this thunder mean? A child crowned like a king!

WITCHES

Be still and listen.

APPARITION

Be of good courage: Glorious and unconquerable shall you be until the wood of Birnam you shall see uproot itself and come towards you!

(*It vanishes.*)

MACBETH

Oh! Happy augury! By magic power never was wood yet made to move.

(*to the Witches*)

Now tell me; shall the progeny of Banquo ever ascend my throne?

WITCHES

Do not ask!

MACBETH

I must know! I must know!
Or my sword shall fall on you.

(*The caldron sinks into the ground.*)

The caldron vanishes! Why?

(*There is a subterranean sound of bagpipes.*)

That music! Speak! What does it mean?

WITCHES

THIRD GROUP

Appear!

SECOND

Appear!

FIRST

Appear!

ALL

Then vanish again like mist.

(*Eight Kings pass by, one after the other; the last, Banquo, with a mirror in his hand.*)

MACBETH

(*to the first*)

Begone, royal specter, you remind me too much of Banquo! The splendor of your diadem sears my eyesight!

(*to the second*)

Away, hideous image with brows bound by a crown!

(*to the others*)

And still others arise?
A third . . . a fourth? . . . a fifth?
Oh, my darkest fears! . . . Now in the hands of the last one I see a mirror shining and other kings arising with-

È Banco! . . . ahi vista orribile!
Ridendo a me gli addita!
Muori, fatal progenie! . . .

(*Trae la spada, savventa agli spettri,*
poi si arretra.)

Ah! chè non hai tu vita!

(*alle Streghe*)

Vivran costor?

STREGHE

Vivranno.

MACBETH

Oh! me perduto!
(*Sviene.*)

STREGHE

Ei svenne!—Aerei spirti,
Ridonate la mente al Re svenuto!
(*Spiriti e Streghe spariscono.*)

MACBETH (*rinviene*)

Ove son io? . . . Svaniro!
. . . Oh sia ne' secoli
Maledetta quest' ora in sempiterno!

(*Entra Lady Macbeth.*)

LADY MACBETH

Vi trovo alfin! Che fate?

MACBETH

Ancora le streghe interrogai!

LADY MACBETH

E disser?

MACBETH

"Da Macduff ti guarda!"

LADY MACBETH

Segui . . .

MACBETH

"Te non ucciderà nato di donna."

LADY MACBETH

Segui . . .

MACBETH

"Invitto sarai finchè la selva di Birnam
contro te non muova."

LADY MACBETH

Segui . . .

MACBETH

Ma pur di Banco apparvemi la stirpe
. . . e regnerà!

LADY MACBETH

Menzogna! Morte, sterminio sull' ini-
qua razza!

MACBETH

Si, morte! di Macduffo arda la rocca!
Perano moglie e prole!

LADY MACBETH

Di Banco il figlio si rinvenga, e muoia!

MACBETH

Tutto il sangue si sperda a noi nemico!

LADY MACBETH

Or riconosco il tuo coraggio antico!

MACBETH

Ora di morte e di vendetta, come assor-
dante l'atro pensiero.

LADY MACBETH

Tuona, rimbomba per l'orbe intero, del
cor le fibre tutte intronò! e di ven-
dette.

LADY MACBETH E MACBETH

Ora di morte omai t'affretta!
Incancellabile il fato ha scritto:
L'impresa compier deve il delitto,
Poichè col sangue s'inaugurò. Vendetta!

ATTO IV

SCENA 1: LUOGO DESERTO AI CONFINI
DELLA SCOZIA E DELL' INGHILTERRA.
IN DISTANZA LA FORESTA DI BIRNAM.

(*Entrano Profughi Scozzesi, Donne,*
Fanciulli. Macduff in disparte ad-
dolorato.)

CORO

Patria oppressa! il dolce nome
No, di madre aver non puoi,
Or che tutta a' figli tuoi
Sei conversa in un avel!

in that magic glass . . . It is Banquo!
. . . Ah, ghastly sight! He smiles as
he shows them to me! Die, fatal
offspring! . . .
(*He draws his sword and rushes
toward the apparitions, but stops.*)
Ah! They have not yet been given life!
(*to the Witches*)
But shall they live?

WITCHES

They shall live.

MACBETH

Oh, I am lost!
(*He swoons.*)

WITCHES

He faints!—Spirits of air, restore
his senses to the fainting King.
(*The Spirits and Witches vanish.*)

MACBETH (*reviving*)

Where am I? . . . they have vanished!
Oh, in all ages may this hour stand
cursed forever!
(*Enter Lady Macbeth.*)

LADY MACBETH

I find you at last! What have you
been doing?

MACBETH

Again I consulted the witches!

LADY MACBETH

What did they say?

MACBETH

"Beware of Macduff!"

LADY MACBETH

And what else . . .

MACBETH

"You will not be killed by a man of
woman born."

LADY MACBETH

And what else . . .

MACBETH

"You will be invincible until the forest
of Birnam shall move against you."

LADY MACBETH

And what else . . .

MACBETH

But yet Banquo's issue appeared to me
and they shall reign!

LADY MACBETH

A lie! Death and destruction on his
hateful tribe!

MACBETH

Yes, death! Macduff's castle shall be
consumed in flames!
His wife and children shall all perish!

LADY MACBETH

Banquo's son shall be recovered and
put to death!

MACBETH

We'll spill the blood of all our enemies!

LADY MACBETH

Now you have recovered your old
courage!

MACBETH

Now death and revenge deafen all
other thoughts.

LADY MACBETH

Thunder, resound throughout the
globe; stun with your sound every
fiber of the soul! Let there be vengeance!

LADY MACBETH AND MACBETH

Now haste apace the hour of death!
Thus immutably Fate has decreed it;
another crime must fulfill our under-
taking, since it was launched in
blood. Vengeance!

ACT IV

SCENE 1: A DESERTED PLACE ON THE
BORDER OF SCOTLAND AND ENGLAND.

*In the distance is the forest of Birnam.
Scottish refugees, women and children; Macduff stands apart, sorrow-
ing.*

CHORUS

Oppressed homeland! No, the dear
name of mother we can no longer
give you now that, for all your children, you are changed into a tomb
of death!

D' orfanelli e di piangenti
Chi lo sposo e chi la prole
Al venir del nuovo Sole
S' alza un grido e fere il Ciel.
A quel grido il Ciel risponde
Quasi voglia impietosito
Propagar per l'infinito,
Patria oppressa, il tuo dolor!
Suona a morto ognor la squilla.
Ma nessuno audace è tanto
Che pur doni un vano pianto
A chi soffre ed a chi muor!

MACDUFF

O figli, o figli miei! Da quel tiranno
Tutti uccisi voi foste, e insiem con voi
La madre sventurata! . . . Ah, fra gli
   artigli
Di quel tigre io lasciai la madre e i figli?
Ah, la paterna mano
Non vi fu scudo, o cari,
Dai perfidi sicari
Che a morte vi ferir!
E me fuggiasco, occulto
Voi chiamavate invano
Coll' ultimo singulto,
Coll' ultimo respir.
Trammi al tiranno in faccia,
Signore! e s' ei mi sfugge,
Possa a colui le braccia
Del tuo perdono aprir.

(A suon di tamburo entra Malcolm
conducendo molti soldati Ingelsi.)

MALCOLM

Dove siam? che bosco è quello?

CORO

La foresta di Birnamo.

MALCOLM

Svelga ognuno e porti un ramo,
Che lo asconda, innanzi a sè.
    (a Macduff)
Ti conforti la vendetta.

MACDUFF

Non l' avrò . . . di figli è privo!

MALCOLM

Chi non odia il suol nativo
Prenda l' armi e segua me.
(Malcolm e Macduff brandendo le
spade)

TUTTI

La patria tradita
Piangendo ne invita!
Fratelli! gli oppressi
Corriamo a salvar.
Già l' ira divina
Sull' empio ruina;
Gli orribili eccessi
L' eterno stancar.

SCEN 2: SCENA NEL CASTELLO DI MAC-
   BETH.

(Notte. Entra un Medico e Dama di
   Lady Macbeth.)

MEDICO

Vegliammo invan due notti.

DAMA

In questa apparirà.

MEDICO

Di che parlava
Nel sonno suo?

DAMA

Ridirlo
Non debbo ad uom che viva . . .
   Eccola! . . .
(Entra lentamente Lady Macbeth son-
   nambula, portando un lume.)

MEDICO

Un lume recasi in man?

DAMA

La lampada che sempre
Si tiene accanto al letto.

MEDICO

Oh come gli occhi spalanca!

DAMA

Eppur non vede.
(Lady Macbeth depone il lume e si
sfrega le mani, facendo l' atto di
cancellare qualche cosa.)

MEDICO

Perchè sfrega le man?

DAMA

Lavarsi crede!

LADY MACBETH

Una macchia è qui tuttora . . .
Via, ti dico, o maledetta!
Una . . . due . . . gli è questa 1 ora!

There is weeping of the bereaved; some
are fathers, some are children. At the
coming of each new dawn there
arises a cry of grief to heaven, to
which cry kind heaven replies as if
with sentiments of pity. We shall
spread, where'er we go, word of your
sorrow, land of woe! The death-knell
everywhere is tolling but none there
are so brave as to offer up a prayer
for those who suffer, those who die.

MACDUFF

O children, my children! You were all
killed by that tyrant, and with you
your poor unfortunate mother! . . .
Ah, and did I leave mother and
children within the claws of that
tiger? Ah, this father's hand was not
there as a shield, my dear ones,
against the pitiless henchmen that
brought death to you! To me, a run-
away, concealed, you called for help
in vain with your last sob, with your
last breath. May I come face to face,
O Lord, with this tyrant! And if he
escapes me, then you may take him
to your embrace and show him pardon.

(With a flourish of trumpets Malcolm
enters, leading troops of English
soldiers.)

MALCOLM

Where are we? What woods are those?

CHORUS

The forest of Birnam.

MALCOLM

Let every man pluck a branch and
carry it before him so that he may
hide himself.

(to Macduff)

Revenge will comfort you.

MACDUFF

Revenge I cannot have . . . he has no
children!

MALCOLM

Whatever man does not despise his
native land, take up arms and follow
me!

(Malcolm and Macduff flourish their
swords.)

ALL

Our fatherland betrayed calls to us
with voice of woe! Brothers in arms!
We run to rescue the oppressed. Now
for sure the wrath divine will bring
down ruin on the villain; now heaven
will exhaust the horrible excesses of
his crimes.

SCENE 2: A HALL IN MACBETH'S CASTLE

It is night time; enter a Physician and
Lady Macbeth's Lady-in-Attendance.

PHYSICIAN

For two nights we have kept watch in
vain.

LADY

Tonight she will appear.

PHYSICIAN

What does she speak of in her sleep?

LADY

I cannot repeat it to any man living . . .
Lo, here she comes! . . .
(Lady Macbeth enters slowly, walking
in her sleep. She carries a candle.)

PHYSICIAN

She has a light in her hand?

LADY

It is the candle that she has always
burning beside her bed.

PHYSICIAN

See how her eyes are sparkling!

LADY

And yet she does not see.
(Lady Macbeth puts down the candle
and rubs her hands, making the
gesture of washing them.)

PHYSICIAN

Why does she rub her hands?

LADY

She thinks she is washing them!

LADY MACBETH

There is still a spot there . . .
Begone, I say, cursed spot!
One . . . two . . . this is the appointed
hour!

Tremi tu? . . . non osi entrar?
Un guerrier così codardo? ?
Oh vergogna! . . . orsù t' affretta!
Chi poteva in quel vegliardo
Tanto sangue immaginar?

MEDICO
Che parlò?

LADY MACBETH
Di Fiffe il Sire
Sposo e padre or non era?
Che ne avvenne? . . .

DAMA E MEDICO
Oh, terror!

LADY MACBETH
. . . E mai pulire
Queste mani io non saprò?

DAMA E MEDICO
Oh, terror!

LADY MACBETH
Di sangue umano
Sa qui sempre . . . Arabia intera
Rimondar sì piccol mano
Co' suoi balsami non può.
Ohimè! . . .

MEDICO
Geme?

LADY MACBETH
I panni indossa
Della notte . . . Oh via ti sbratta!
Banco è spento, e dalla fossa
Chi morì non surse ancor.

MEDICO
Questo ancor? . . .

LADY MACBETH
A letto, a letto . . .
Sfar non puoi la cosa fatta . . .
Batte alcuno! . . . andiam, Macbetto,
Non t' accusi il tuo pallor.

DAMA E MEDICO
Ah di lei pietà!

SCENA 3: SALA NEL CASTELLO

(Entra Macbeth.)

Perfidi! All' Anglo contro me v' unite!
Le potenze presaghe han profetato:

"Esser puoi sanguinario, feroce;
"Nessun nato di donna ti nuoce."
No, non temo di voi, nè del fanciullo
Che vi conduce! Raffermar sul trono
Questo assalto mi debbe,
O sbalzarmi per sempre! . . . Eppur la vita
Sento nelle mie fibre inaridita!
Pietà, rispetto, amore,
Conforto a' di cadenti,
Ah! non spargeran d' un fiore
La tua canuta età.
Nè sul tuo regio sasso
Sperar soavi accenti;
Ah! sol la bestemmia, ahi lasso!
Sol la nenia tua sarà

DONNE *(nell' interno)*
Ella è morta!

MACBETH
Qual gemito!
(Entra Dama di Lady Macbeth.)

DAMA
È morta la Regina.

MACBETH
(con indifferenza e sprezzo)
La vita! . . . che importa?
È il racconto d' un povero idiota,
Vento e suono che nulla dinota.
*(Dama parte. Entra Coro di Guerrieri
di Macbeth.)*

CORO
Sire! Ah, Sire!

MACBETH
Che fu? . . . quali nuove?

CORO
La foresta di Birnam si muove!

MACBETH
(attonito)
M' hai deluso, infernale presagio! . . .
Qui l' usbergo, la spada, il pugnale!
Prodi, all' armi! La morte! o la vittoria!

CORO
Dunque all' armi! La morte, o la vittoria.
*(Suono interno de trombe. Intanto la
scena si muta, e presenta una vasta
pianura. Il fondo è occupato da*

You tremble? . . . Do you not dare go in?

A warrior and thus afraid?

Oh, shame! . . . Come, hurry!

Who could have imagined there was so much blood in that old man?

PHYSICIAN

What is she saying?

LADY MACBETH

The Thane of Fife was a husband and a father or was he not? Whatever became of him?

LADY AND PHYSICIAN

Oh, horror!

LADY MACBETH

And shall I never know these hands to be clean again?

LADY AND PHYSICIAN

Oh, horror!

LADY MACBETH

Forever tinged with human blood . . .

All Arabia with its perfumes can not cleanse this little hand.

Alas! . . .

PHYSICIAN

She sighs.

LADY MACBETH

Put on your night clothes . . .

Come on, get out of here!

Banquo is snuffed out and the dead cannot rise again from the grave.

PHYSICIAN

That theme again.

LADY MACBETH

To bed . . . to bed . . .

What's done cannot be undone . . .

Someone's knocking! . . Let us go, Macbeth, lest your pallid looks accuse you.

LADY AND PHYSICIAN

Heaven have mercy on her!

SCENE 3: A BATTLEFIELD

Macbeth is deep in thought.

MACBETH

Traitors! To unite against me with the English! Those potent seers did prophesy:

"Be fierce and bloody; for none born of woman can harm you."

No, I have no fear of you nor of the boy who leads you on! For this assault must either confirm me on my throne or else unseat me forever! And yet I feel my life grow dry within my frame! Kindness, respect and love, the comforts of declining days, will not scatter a flower to cheer your frosty age, nor breathe soft words upon your royal tomb. Ah! Curses alone are left to you, alas! Curses alone will be your epitaph.

WOMEN'S VOICES

She is dead!

MACBETH

What cry is this?

(*Enter Lady Macbeth's Lady-in-Attendance.*)

LADY

The Queen is dead!

MACBETH

(*with indifference and scorn*)

Life!

. . . what does it matter?

It is the tale of a poor idiot, wind and sound that mean nothing.

(*Exit Lady. A chorus of Macbeth's warriors enters.*)

CHORUS

Sire! Your majesty!

MACBETH

What is it? . . . What is your news?

CHORUS

Birnam forest is on the move!

MACBETH (*astounded*)

You have deluded me . . . infernal prophets!

Give me my breastplate, sword and dagger!

To arms, brave men! To death or victory!

CHORUS

Then every man to arms! To death or victory!

(*There is a sound of trumpets within. Meanwhile the scene changes and becomes an open plain. The background is filled with English soldiers*

soldati Inglesi, i quali lentamente si avanzono, portando ciascheduno una fronda innanzi a sè.)

(Entra Malcolm, Macduff e Soldati.)

MACDUFF

Via le fronde, e mano all' armi!
Mi seguite!

SOLDATI

All' armi! all' armi!

(Malcolm e Soldati partono.)

MACDUFF

Carnefice de' figli miei, t' ho giunto!

MACBETH

Fuggi! nato di donna
Uccidermi non può.

MACDUFF

Nato non sono: strappato
Fui dal sen materno.

MACBETH

Cielo!

(Brandiscono le spade e disperatmente combattono. Macbeth cade.)

MACBETH

(Si alza a poco a poco da terra.)

Mal per me che m' affidai
Ne' presagi dell' inferno!
Tutto il sangue ch' io versai
Grida in faccia dell' Eterno! . . .
Sulla fronte . . . maledetta! . . .
Sfolgorò . . . la sua vendetta!
Muoio . . . al Cielo . . . al mondo in
    ira.
Vil corona! . . . e sol per te!

(Muore.)

CORO

Vittoria!

(Entra Malcolm seguito da soldati Inglesi, i quali trascinano prigioneri quelli di Macbeth. Macduff con altri Soldati, Bardi e Popolo.)

MALCOLM

Ove s'è fitto l'usurpator?

MACDUFF

Colà da me trafitto.
(piegando un ginocchio a terra)
Salve, o Re!

CORO

Salve, o Re!

BARDI

Macbetto ov'e? dov'è l'usurpator?
D'un soffio il fulmino,
D'un soffio il Dio della vittoria.

(a Macduff)

Il prode eroe egl' è .che spense il
    traditor!
La patria, il Re salvò; a lui onor e
    gloria!

DONNE

Salgan mie grazie a te,
Gran Dio vendicator;
A chi ne liberò
Inni cantiam di gloria.

MACDUFF

S' affidi ognun al Re
Ridato al nostro amor!
L' aurora che spuntò
Vi darà pace e gloria!

MALCOLM

Confida, o Scozia, in me;
Fu spento l' oppressor!
La gioia eternerò
Per noi di tal vittoria!

FINE DELL' OPERA

who advance slowly forward, each man covered by a tree branch that he holds in front of him.)

(Enter Malcolm, Macduff and soldiers.)

MACDUFF

Throw down your boughs and take your swords in hand!
Follow me!

SOLDIERS

To arms! To arms!
(Exit Malcolm and soldiers.)

MACDUFF

Butcher of my children, at last I have found you!

MACBETH

Begone, for no man born of woman can harm me.

MACDUFF

I was not born; I was torn from my mother's womb.

MACBETH

Oh, heaven!

(They brandish swords and fight furiously. Macbeth falls. Macduff rushes off.)

MACBETH

(Little by little he manages to raise himself from the ground.)
Evil the day when I did trust the prophecies I heard from hell!
Now all the blood that I have spilled cries out to heaven against me! . . .
Upon my head . . . a curse! . . .
Like lightning it falls . . . in vengeance:
I die . . . hated by heaven and earth.
Vile crown! . . . it was all for thee!
(He dies.)

CHORUS

Victory!

(Enter Malcolm and English soldiers who drag in Macbeth's followers as prisoners. Macduff enters with other soldiers, countrymen and populace.)

MALCOLM

Where has the usurper got to?

MACDUFF

There he lies, slain by my sword.
(He kneels.)
Long live the King!

CHORUS

Long live the King!

COUNTRYMEN

Where is Macbeth? Wheere is the usurper?
Struck down by a bolt of thunder, by a blow from the god of victory.

(to Macduff)

He is the valiant hero who requited the traitor!
Both King and country saved; to him all honor and glory!

WOMEN

Our grateful prayers arise
To Thee, O God of retribution.
Hymns of praise we sing
To him who set us free.

MACDUFF

Let every man confide
In our returned and much beloved King.
The dawn which new is breaking
Will bring us peace and glory.

MALCOLM

Scotland, trust in me;
The oppressor is overthrown!
Our joy in this great victory
Will remain with us forever.

END OF THE OPERA